Seven Lonely Places

Seven Warm Places

the Vices and Virtues for children

Written by April Bolton ★ Illustrated by Brent Beck

ST. ANTHONY MESSENGER PRESS

Cincinnati, Ohio

Book design by Mark Sullivan

Library of Congress Cataloging-in-Publication Data

Bolton, April, 1943–

 Seven lonely places, seven warm places : the vices and virtues for
children / by April Bolton ; illustrations by Brent Beck.
     p. cm.
Summary: Simple text describes what it can be like to commit the seven
deadly sins, such as greed being followed by an empty feeling, and to
live seven virtues, such as knowing that God will make things better
when one has hope.
 ISBN 0-86716-482-4
 1. Deadly sins—Juvenile literature. 2. Cardinal virtues—Juvenile
literature. [1. Sins. 2. Virtues. 3. Conduct of life.] I. Beck, Brent,
ill. II. Title.
 BV4626 .B65 2002
 241'.3 dc21

                                        2002014658

ISBN 0-86716-482-4
Published by St. Anthony Messenger Press
www.AmericanCatholic.org
Printed in the U.S.A.

For a Grown-up:

Sin is lonely. And children understand "lonely."

In addition to the bad effects our sins have on other people, our sins have bad effects on us. Sin puts us in places where we are alone—places we don't want to be. Sin removes us from God, puts us in places where we can't see God's face or feel God's presence.

Virtue is warm. And children understand being warm, feeling love and feeling loved.

In addition to the good effects that our acts of virtue have on other people, our acts of virtue have good effects on us. We all know the warm feeling we get when something we have done or said makes another person feel good. Perhaps we have then felt God's presence and are experiencing the certainty that God is Love.

Children and adults don't like to be told to do something, or not do something, "because I said so." As we grow older we learn to listen if we hear that we are to do something, or not to do something, "because God says so." But this knowledge comes with experience of the wisdom of our church's teaching, of God's teaching, which children do not always have. How many years of contemplation and experience does it take to understand the truth of the Beatitudes, or the truth of our faith, that "it is in giving that we receive"?

Children are fresh in the world and new to the teachings of our God and our church. They operate on a more immediate level. They may hear what you say to them, and they may successfully parrot back to you what you have said, but they secretly believe in and rely on their own experience more than on any words they have heard. They rely on what they have seen and felt. They *do* know the explosive feelings of anger, and they *do* know the feeling of having turned on a light in a dark room.

If, with children, we approach sin and virtue in an immediate fashion, they are more likely to understand and to absorb our admonitions to avoid the seven deadly, or capital, sins, and to cultivate the four cardinal and three theological virtues.

Seven
Lonely
Places

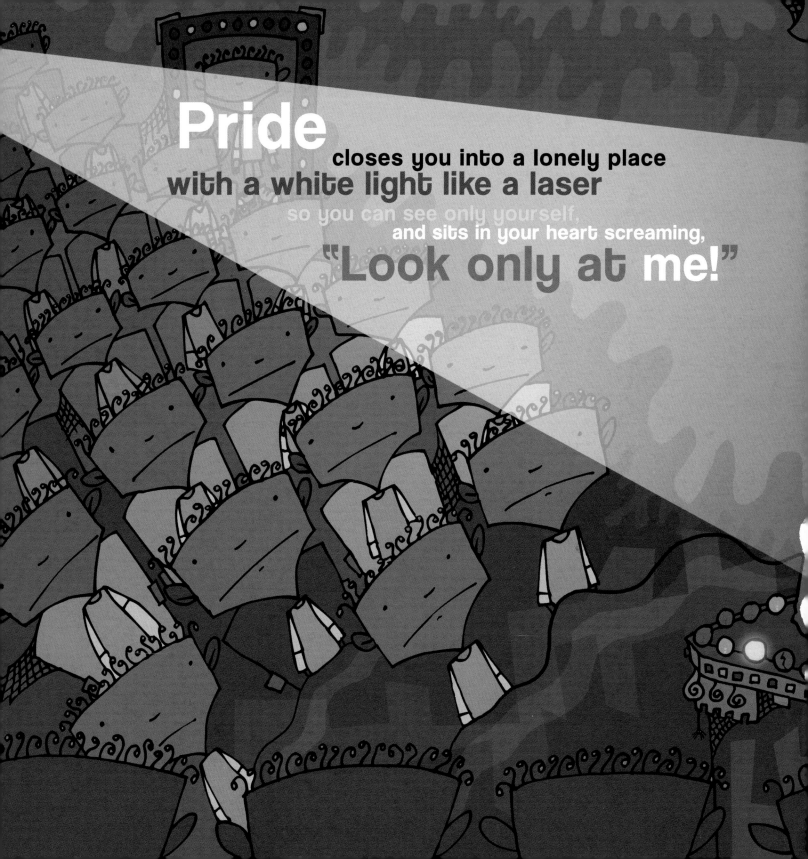

Pride closes you into a lonely place
with a white light like a laser
so you can see only yourself,
and sits in your heart screaming,
"Look only at me!"

Envy

is a foggy place like a deep **dark** swamp
where **what you have** shrinks and fades
and what your friend has grows **big** and **bright**
so what you have is not enough and you want what your friend has.
What **you** have becomes dim as **shadows**.

Anger

scrunches your heart into a tiny lump of charcoal
and bursts all your insides out
before you know what happens.
Then you look around empty and all alone.

Lust makes you say,
"I will take you for my pleasure to make **me** feel good.
Who cares what you think?"
Lust is a world of only one person
and all the other people are toys and not real!

Gluttony

is a big wide hole that you can't fill up.
Gluttony makes you look at the box of chocolate chip cookies and think,

'Yes, yes, yes...they must all go not beside me,
not next to me, but inside me.
The whole world belongs inside me.'

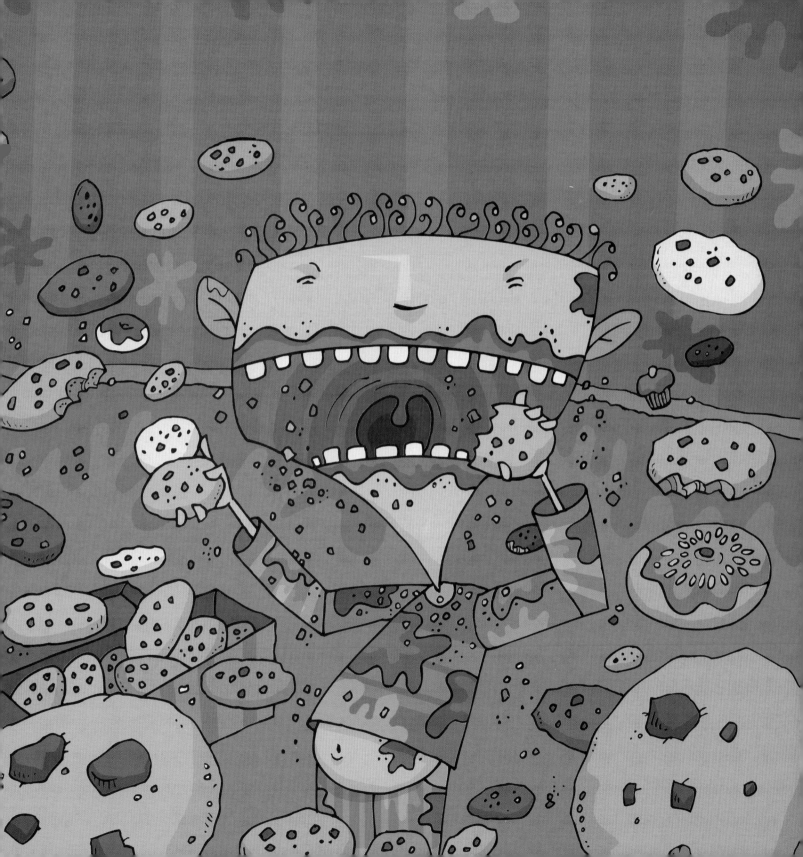

Sloth
tells you to say, "Nah, I won't do it.
I'll let someone else do it, because I don't want to
and my foot hurts and I'm real tired."

And, "Be quiet, voices that tell me to do things. Nothing is important."
Sloth makes you think the world outside you isn't even there.

These are seven lonely places.

Seven
Warm
Places

Prudence

lights your room

**so you can see how to pick up your toys and hang up your clothes
and how to shut your mouth when you want to yell at someone.**

Prudence looks out

at what you can do to make the world better

and does it!

Justice
divides your peanut butter sandwich
into a zillion parts
for the children who don't have any lunch.
Justice is the place where you see
everyone must have what they need.

Courage
takes up where others leave off crying
and goes into the dark place
to turn on the light.

Faith

lifts the latch to your mind

so that you know God is there

and that every little bit counts.

With **hope**
you see the bad things in the world
and you **see** how **God** will help you
make them **better!**

Charity

opens the door to your h**e**a**r**t
and says, **"He hurt me,**
but one . . . two . . . three . . . four . . . five . . .
he must be hurting, too, and I love him."
Charity tells you God loves you.

These places are filled with light.

These are the seven gifts
God gives us
to help us move out of
the seven lonely places.

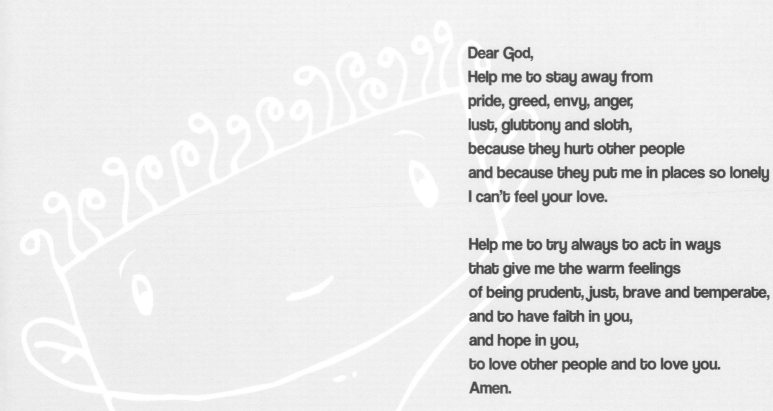

Dear God,
Help me to stay away from
pride, greed, envy, anger,
lust, gluttony and sloth,
because they hurt other people
and because they put me in places so lonely
I can't feel your love.

Help me to try always to act in ways
that give me the warm feelings
of being prudent, just, brave and temperate,
and to have faith in you,
and hope in you,
to love other people and to love you.
Amen.